How To WOO Her
A Romantic Idea Guide for Guys

By Jaime T. McLain

Edited by Erica Agiewich

Illustrated by Douglas Berdeaux

Copyright © 2015 Jaime T. McLain

All rights reserved.

ISBN: 1516826310
ISBN-13: 9781516826315

DEDICATION

To Jay, Angela and Samantha

Know that I try very hard to be a good man and a good father. Remember that true love is rare but so worth the struggle when you find it. Be good to yourselves and each other. I love all of you so much and I am always here for you.

&

Princess

You are the most amazing woman I have ever known. Thank you for everything. In time your struggles will subside and the life of happiness and love that you deserve will follow you always. Here's to a life filled with romance and "wow's".

CONTENTS

	Acknowledgments	i
1	Introduction	Pg 1
2	Background	Pg 3
3	Flowers Can Be So Boring	Pg 7
4	Fairytale Princess	Pg 13
5	Life is a Song	Pg 17
6	Love Nest	Pg 21
7	Facebook	Pg 25
8	Movie Night	Pg 29
9	The Light of My Life	Pg 35
10	Dance the Night Away	Pg 39
11	Summer Picnic	Pg 43
12	Massage	Pg 47
13	The Notebook	Pg 57
14	Open When	Pg 61
15	What's in a Label?	Pg 65

CONTENTS

16	Puzzle Pieces	Pg 69
17	Hammock	Pg 73
18	Cooking	Pg 77
19	Dining Out	Pg 85
20	Scavenger Hunt	Pg 95
21	Gifts	Pg 99
22	Bedroom Romance	Pg 103
23	Conclusion	Pg 107
	About the Author	Pg 111
	Reference	Pg 113

Jaime T. McLain

ACKNOWLEDGMENTS

I need to acknowledge first and foremost the woman that made this all possible, Sang Eetha. She is the most caring and loving person that I have ever met. When she should have run from me she instead grew closer and became my best friend even while struggling with her own challenges. After reading this you will undoubtedly know how incredible she is and how lucky I am to have met her. My hope is that at some point in their life, every man will experience the unconditional love and friendship that I have experienced with her.

Next would be my children who never thought less of me even in my darkest times. Jay became my closest friend when I needed one the most, Angela who grew up so fast and went through so much more than she should have had to and of course Samantha, the one who only sees the good in people. They may never realize how spending time with them is the highlight of my life and how much I look forward to it.

I also want to thank Lisa for listening to me babble on like a school kid in love and helping me come up with many of these ideas. I also need to thank the two partners in crime, Stacia and Min, for looking out for me when I needed it and doing everything they could to make sure these dates went perfect. I need to thank Revathi as well. She listened to me when she didn't need to, taught me so much about culture and the language, who refused to give up on me when she should have and ultimately suggested that I write this. Lastly I a special thank you to Douglas Berdeaux who went above and beyond on the illustration and actually "wow'd" me.

Jaime T. McLain

1 INTRODUCTION

What is this book? While thinking about what this book is, my first thought is what this book isn't. I think from there I can go into what this book is. First of all this book is not a dating guide. This is not going to help someone pick up a girl. This is not a "hook up" guide and is not designed to get someone into bed. This is not a good guide to use if you do not know your partner very well or have just recently met them. Lastly I do not know if this would be good advice to use on the same gender since I have no experience with that but I don't see why it wouldn't. I have used these on one amazing woman and they yielded great results.

So what is this book? This is simply a collection of ideas that I have used to show my feelings for the woman I love. Some of these ideas I found on the internet and some I came up with on my own or with the help of friends. This is simply an attempt to put down these ideas in one place in the hope that it may help other people show how they feel and to make someone else feel special. I have actually used more ideas than what I put in this book but only included the ones with a "wow" affect. These came to me from the heart and they should be used in the same way.

Many people struggle with being romantic. For some it just doesn't come naturally and others hold back because out of concern for how their friends would perceive it. Many men want to be the strong silent type. That is great but most women would like to see the romantic side come out once in a while. Hopefully this book will help some people to be more romantic and to help build a solid, loving relationship that continues to grow for years to come.

The most precious gifts are ones that come from your heart and not my heart, so I encourage you to use this as a guide and modify any of these ideas to fit your specific relationship. Reach into your heart and make these personal to you and your partner. Try to come up with ideas of your own. After all, it is the feelings that she has created inside of you that have caused you to want to do special things for her.

2 BACKGROUND

So my story starts after the end of a twenty-four year marriage. It was the darkest time of my life and I wish that nobody else would ever have to go through that pain. The good news is that according to the New York Times, divorce rates in the United States have actually gone down and marriages are lasting longer today than they were several years ago, but there is still a 45% chance of a marriage ending in divorce (Miller, 2014). There is hope however. As you can see from the chart below, people that were married in the 2000's are trending in a more positive direction. Perhaps we are finally finding a way to keep the love and romance alive in a relationship.

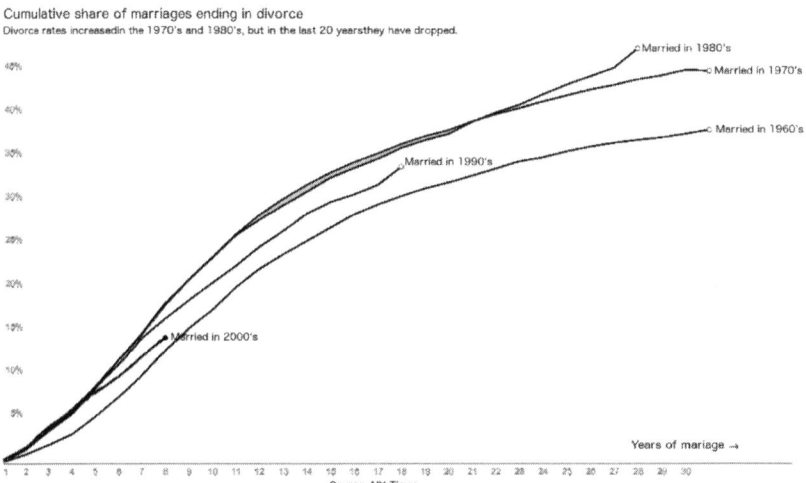

My marriage was certainly not perfect but I thought I was going to grow old with her and we'd spend the rest of our life together. We were high school sweethearts that got married very young but I really thought we were going to make it. It can be very difficult to carry on after everything that you thought you knew to be true and right comes to an end.

To help me cope, I joined a divorce support group. I gained comfort from the group in knowing that I was not the only person that felt this terrible and, in fact, other people hurt after a long term breakup as well. The group was approximately half men and half women which also helped me understand that men were painfully affected by divorce too. This was foreign to me since I was raised to believe that men should be strong and silent.

It was in this group that I met the person that would change my life and be the inspiration for these ideas and, ultimately, this book. We began as friends who leaned on and respected each other during rough periods. That friendship grew into attraction and ultimately love.

I think it's important for my readers to understand the type of connection that was required to create this outpouring of ideas and emotions -- especially since I was not known for this previously. So who is this person that I keep referring to? This person came into my life at the worst possible time for a relationship and wound up becoming my closest friend. It really started off in the most innocent way. In the support group we were assigned a person that we were to call on a daily basis to check on them and talk about anything that was bothering us. The assigned partners didn't take to well with our group but over time the natural selection of friends started to form, mine was with her. We had a friendship connection from the beginning and started confiding in each other about the most personal of things. We would call each other when we were not having a good day or were emotional and help the other person get through it. Sometimes just listening is the most important thing a friend can do and it means so much. It was comforting to have someone safe to call and be able to discuss what was bothering us without having to worry about how it would be taken or having to be careful about what we said. Listening to your most personal feelings and not judging you is the sign of a true friend and a very rare find.

I remember being so nervous when I finally asked her out on a date even though I had dated other women since I had separated from my wife. I can't really explain it but this woman was different. I bring this up because I think it is pertinent to the use and purpose of this book. These ideas came from the heart and exist because of her. That's why I recommend using this for that special someone, not the special someone right now. This is best used for partner that gives you butterflies when you see her; that makes you want to clean the house or wash the car or make everything perfect before you go out with her because the feelings that you have for her are that strong. You know when you change outfits three times before going on a date with her? Yeah, that kind of woman. This is a feeling that doesn't happen often. In fact many people experience this only once in a lifetime and some not at all.

Take this book and use it as a guide to make your woman feel special. If she is that special then she deserves to feel that way from you. Your relationship should never grow old and only the two of you can prevent that. Continue to come up with new ideas and ways that you can keep that fire alive. A strong solid relationship between two people that truly love each other is a beautiful thing that deserves to be nurtured.

For the people on the receiving end of these ideas, please understand that expressing these kinds of emotions can be very difficult for some people and it may be a big deal for them to do these ideas. Enjoy them but never take them for granted, even if they do them too often or not quite perfect because each one means a lot to them. Take them as they are meant to be, with love and affection to someone very special to him.

3 FLOWERS CAN BE SO BORING

What You'll Need

- Flowers
- Dinner Reservations

Every woman that I have known loves flowers but it can get boring if all you do is pick some up on your way home from work. Don't get me wrong, that has its place but it certainly isn't "wowing" your partner. The answer is not to stop getting flowers for them. Why would you stop doing something that brings so much joy to her? The answer is to come up with new and creative ideas that involve flowers. There are endless ways to give your partner flowers and I encourage you to reach into your heart and come up with some of your own.

One of my favorite things to do is to have flowers delivered to the restaurant table during dinner. Many of my friends say that dinner is not appropriate for flowers because once they are given, they can be cumbersome and take a lot of table space away but judging from the reaction of my girlfriend, I think otherwise.

You also need to know the meaning of the different flowers. You give her flowers for a certain affect and you certainly do not want to project something that was not intended. Roses are the most commonly given flowers but there are many more types of flowers that are beautiful in a bouquet. Carnations, lilies, wild flowers, tulips and daisies are just a few others to consider.

Lets start with roses since they are the most commonly given flower to show love. First there is the type of bouquet. A single rose is elegant and shows her how much you care about her. This is a good option if you are on a budget since a dozen long stem roses can cost more than $50. Carrying a dozen long stem roses all evening can be a chore so it's also a good choice if you will be out and away from anyplace that she conveniently can leave the flowers. The next option is to get roses that are part of a larger bouquet. These mixed bouquets can be very beautiful and they soften the meaning of the roses. A dozen long stem red roses is the standard for an "I love you" bouquet, but a half dozen roses mixed in with carnations and other flowers is a little less serious. This is a good choice for a young relationship that has not developed to the "I love you" stage. It's also good for less meaningful events or to give them just because you were thinking about her. The last way is to give a traditional dozen roses. When given the option, always go for long stem roses because woman have been taught that it means more to get long stem roses as opposed to the cheaper shorter stem variety. It may not make sense to pay the extra money for them since she is only going to cut the stems so she can put them in a vase but this isn't about logic. Remember that this book is called "How To Wow Your Partner", not "How To Mediocre Your Partner". A dozen long stem roses is the choice for special occasions. This is good for anniversaries or asking that special question.

Roses come in many different colors and each color has a distinct meaning. There are some generally accepted meanings for the different colors and it is important to know the difference so that you are conveying the correct message.

- **Red** – Red is for love. If you are not ready or willing to say "I love you" then avoid red roses. There simply is no other meaning of a red rose then I love you.
- **Pink** – Pink says "I am starting to have romantic feelings for you." This is a good choice if you have not progressed to the stage in your relationship where you are openly telling each other that you are in love.
- **Yellow** – Yellow symbolizes friendship. Yellow roses are great to give a friend or to give a girlfriend early in your relationship. This is a good choice for a first date (provided that you have known each other prior to this date).
- **White** – White roses show sympathy, purity and innocence. Use white roses for weddings or engagement events, not for your sweetheart. These are too cold to be used to show her you have romantic feelings.

After roses I find that carnations are good option for flowers. They are readily available, inexpensive, come in may different colors and are very beautiful. The meanings of the various colors of carnations mirror those of roses so for example, a yellow carnation would be given as a show of friendship while a red carnation would show love. Carnations are a good way to show that you love someone. I find them very useful to use between the times that I give roses. While roses are great for special occasions, carnations can be given anytime. Bouquets of carnations of mixed colors can be very pretty and look great as a dinner table centerpiece.

Wild flowers are great to give spontaneously. Go for a walk or plan a picnic (Chapter 9) and pick some while you are out. Wild flowers will save you on the costs of flowers but be sure that you are allowed to pick them. Many places have them protected from being picked or they may be on private property. This is a nice spontaneous way to be romantic and let her know that you are enjoying your time with her. While they don't scream love, they do show that you have feelings for her. Wild flowers win high points for the spontaneity and are very beautiful. Also there is little concern about rushing home to put them in a vase since they were free.

The other types of flowers such as lilies, daisies, tulips and other more unique flowers such as birds of paradise can be used at various times but keep in mind that they do not project the feeling of love like roses and carnations do. They are best used for table displays or as fillers to create a stunning and different looking bouquet. If you are invited over to her place for dinner you can choose these types flowers as a thank you gift for the table. If she is coming to your place for dinner you should have some of these on your table. I can't tell you how many times I have been told by a woman that they love a man that has fresh flowers at his house. Of course I don't have them all the time but I certainly do when I know she is coming over. It shows that you are a caring person with a sensitive side to you. It also tells her that you have a sense of style and that you most likely have more in your closet than old concert t-shirts.

So now that you have chosen your flowers what will you do with them? One of my favorite things to do is to present flowers at dinner. Some people recommend no flowers at dinner because then she has to carry them the rest of the night. But if it is a dinner with just the two of you I think it works very well. To have the biggest effect you need the element of surprise. To accomplish this you will need to arrive at the restaurant early. Just a few minutes early works if you are meeting her there but if you are picking her up you'll need to drop them off at the restaurant first.

At the restaurant you should talk to the hostess or a manager about your plan. They usually are very good at this and usually seem excited to help. I usually tip them to ensure that it gets done and to say thank you. Ask them to bring the flowers to the table after the appetizer but before the main course because you want to get settled in first. If they bring them too soon the effect will be diminished with the focus being put on sitting down, reviewing the menu, ordering, etc. After the appetizer you and your partner will have most likely had some of your drinks already and started to engage in conversation. This combined with the natural lull that exists between the courses will make a nice effect. It also gives enough time left at dinner for you to enjoy the closeness that will ultimately happen after she receives the flowers. Don't be surprised if some of the employees stop by to comment on how pretty they are and what a great guy you are. The certainly helps raise you up to new levels in her eyes.

For an added touch, when you setup the delivery of the flowers with the restaurant staff have them place your favorite bottle of wine, or whatever your partners favorite drink is, already on the table when you arrive. This will get her thinking that you took the time to call ahead and encourage her thinking romantic thoughts about you. Finally when all of this is setup, you need to leave the restaurant and come back with her so that it appears that you are just arriving for the first time with her.

When the two of you arrive at the restaurant try really hard to not give it away until the flowers arrive. She'll know something is up when she see's the wine already on the table but it will be truly magical when the flowers are delivered.

Jaime T. McLain

4 FAIRYTALE PRINCESS

What You'll Need

- A company that offers horse drawn carriage rides
- Dinner Reservations
- Blanket
- Favorite drink (optional)

I am the father of two girls and the brother to four sisters so I have learned a little about what women think about and what triggers different emotions for them. Many women fantasize about being a princess and falling in love with the prince. I have yet to meet a woman that did not grow up playing princess, wearing tiaras and watching Disney movies about princesses. This fantasy life is engrained into them at an early age and why not? Many are great stories of the prince that fights for the heart of their princess. They are stories about life in a castle, wearing gorgeous jewelry and having a wonderfully romantic life. Just look at the media coverage of the royal family events in England. Every social event that they attend, whenever one gets married, has a child or basically anything they do gets massive media coverage. This is because of the pageantry and the fairytale that they inspire in people.

So what can a guy do to compete against the fantasy? You can create your own fairytale right where you live. To do this you will need to spend some time on the internet finding a company or nearby horse farm that provides carriage rides. Many large cities have events that they come out to but it may be difficult to find them in smaller towns. For example, there may be a heritage fair or spring fling downtown where they offer carriage rides. In my town it was a winter festival advertisement that caught my eye. They were offering horse drawn carriage rides during the event so I looked up the company and gave them a call. These companies usually take you for a ride through downtown or through a large park such as Central Park.

Schedule the event with the company and agree on a time and location. If it is cold out you may want to bring a blanket. I scheduled it in November and it was chilly, but luckily the company provided a nice warm blanket. This is a good excuse to cuddle up together as well. You can bring drinks and, in my case, I prepared hot chocolate for the ride. Whatever drink you prepare, always use the best. No powders here. You don't want to spend all of this time and money to setup the perfect evening just to serve some generic powder drink.

Before the carriage ride, I recommend starting the evening with a nice dinner. Choose someplace nice, remember this is a fairytale evening not an evening on a budget. If you can, choose a restaurant near the location that the carriage ride will start and see if they will pick you up at the restaurant. Remember that the only thing better than being treated like a princess is to be treated like a princess with everyone watching. I have found that even woman that typically do not like to be the center of attention do enjoy some attention when it's done in a positive and respectful way such as this. If for some reason picking you up at the restaurant is not an option, try and walk to the pickup location. It will give you a chance to talk and connect more before the big event.

Remember to not say anything throughout the night about this. You want this is be a great night with the carriage ride being the climax of a perfect evening. When you are ready to meet the carriage, you might want to look at her and say something along the lines of, "Is my princess ready for her fairytale?" If you time this perfectly the horse and carriage will come into sight immediately after you ask her.

When the horse and carriage arrives, help her into the buggy. Remember that you are now her prince and you need to treat her like a princess. Once seated it may be appropriate to give her a kiss, after all she will be thinking that you are the greatest guy ever at this point. Now bring out the blanket and cuddle up to your princess. She will want to get very close to her prince at this point. Try to keep the conversation to a minimum during the ride. Small talk is fine but let her enjoy the moment. Every girl that see's you will be jealous and look at her guy with the "why don't you do things like that" look. Let your princess enjoy the spotlight for this fantasy come true moment.

Jaime T. McLain

5 LIFE IS A SONG

What You'll Need

- A Karaoke bar or restaurant

Women love when feelings and actions come from the heart. It's more about the thought and the outpouring of affection than the actual execution. That doesn't mean that you shouldn't do everything you can to make the event as perfect as possible, but what it does mean is that you should not avoid one of these ideas simply because you feel you are not good at it. The fact that you tried something that you knew you would not be good at or that made you feel uncomfortable doing just to show her how you feel about her will win you high praise from her. This is one of those ideas that may make you feel uncomfortable but will blow her away.

There are many songs that have been written over the years about the love that the writer feels for someone. Some famous examples are *Layla* and *Wonderful Tonight* by Eric Clapton, *I Have To Say I Love You In A Song* by Jim Croce, *When I See You Smile* by Bad English and even *Sweet Child O' Mine* by Guns N' Roses. Unfortunately most of us do not have the talent needed to write a hit love song but with so many of them out there, there are plenty of existing ones for us to choose from to express our feelings. Make sure you choose a song that represents your relationship. For example, *Sister Golden Hair* by America may not be appropriate if she is a brunette. When I did this I sang *When I See You Smile* by Bad English because I think she has the most beautiful smile and thinking about it had helped me through some pretty rough times. So pick something that makes you think of her or perhaps talks about something you two have experienced together.

While not necessary, I took a couple of singing lessons prior to attempting karaoke. I'm not sure if it helped much but I am such a bad singer I knew any help would be beneficial. I looked up singing lessons on Craigslist and found someone local that seemed knowledgeable, nice and understanding about what I was trying to do. While the quality of my voice did not change, the instructor helped me a lot with inflection, singing with feeling and singing to the audience. Remember guys, it's more about the fact that you took the time to do it and the feelings that you are conveying then the quality of your singing. Even though karaoke places the words on a screen for you, take the time to learn the lyrics. The one thing that can ruin all of this work is to stumble on stage and not know the words. I added the song to playlist in my car and listened to it for a few days prior just to learn the words and how it was sung.

You'll need to make sure that the karaoke place has the song that you want to sing, especially if it's not a commonly played song. You can stop in a few days before your big event or do what I did and call ahead and talk to the DJ about the plan. He loved the idea and when I introduced myself the night of the event he was almost as excited as I was. We set it up so that he would look for me to give him a signal when I was ready. It can also help lessen your fears if you bring some friends along. You might think that this could make you more nervous but if they are aware of your plan they can sing along and get the audience into it. In my case, once the audience realized I was singing to a special girl, they started singing with me and gave me high-fives when I was done.

When they call your name to come on stage the jig is up, but that's good because this is what you have been preparing for. Above all else, remember to sing to her. It helps if you have found a table near the stage or at least have her come up near you while you are singing. Look her in the eyes and gesture towards her. When the song talks about love or heart, look at her and place your hand over your heart to show her that all of this is about your affection for her. Remember that we are not professional singers so the real wow factor comes from you singing to her, not the quality of your singing. It does you no good to set all of this up and then sing to the audience and not her. She is your entire audience for this performance.

When you are done and come off of the stage, be prepared for a very emotional woman. She may be crying a bit but don't worry, they are tears of joy. In my case, she held onto me the rest of the evening like I was a lifeboat on the Titanic. Congratulations, you have just created a memory in that woman that will last a lifetime and she will be telling all of her friends about it for a very long time.

Jaime T. McLain

6 LOVE NEST

What You'll Need

- Blankets
- Comforters
- Pillows
- Folder clips
- String
- Internet capable television (optional)

The Love Nest or Cuddle Fort was one of the most successful date nights in this book. In fact, she made me promise to do it again! The idea came to me as I was cleaning the house in preparation for a date at home that evening. The evening was just supposed to be a simple dinner but it ended up being so much more.

Remember when you were a kid and you built a fort out of an old cardboard box or maybe it was a small tent in the back yard. These places provide a feeling of comfort and safety that will allow your partner to feel at ease and bring them closer to you. It will help them forget about the stresses of being an adult for a short while and bring them back to a time in their lives when everything was fun and there wasn't as much to stress about.

The great thing about building a love fort is that you should have most, if not all of the needed items already around the house. You'll need:

- Blankets to use as walls
- Comforters to soften the floor
- Lots of pillows to lean against.
- Kite string to hang the blankets but you can also use the backs of chairs.
- Something to hold the blankets together. For this I used those little black clips that are used to hold documents to folders. They are easy to fine, inexpensive and work great.
- Internet capable television is optional but makes for a nice touch as I'll explain later.

The first thing to do is to find a suitable location to build your love nest. I happened to have a sectional couch that wrapped around in the shape of an L. This created the perfect comfy place to start the fort. Once the location is selected the next step is to build the frame that will support the walls of your nest. I used kite string to support my blankets but get creative and try to make use out of your surroundings and tools already on hand. I used the railing of a nearby staircase to tie one end of the sting to and I used speaker stands from my surround sound system for the other. Just use whatever you have that can hold the blankets. You want to string them like a Tic-tac-toe board. You can use the backs of chairs as well but I found the kite string held the weight of the blankets much better.

Once you have the frame in place it's time to lay out the blankets. Use thin blankets for the walls and ceiling and save the thick ones for floor padding. Since you want to create the feeling of an enclosed space make sure to block out any sunlight that may come in. Lay the blankets over the string on three sides. On the front just lay the blanket slightly over the string with just an inch or two hanging over so that you can have an opening. Since I built mine around a sectional sofa, I was able to lay the bottom of the blankets on the cushions but if you don't have that you'll need to hang them to the floor. Use the folder clips to secure the blankets to the string and to each other to keep them from opening up. Always put the clips on the outside, remember you will both be on the inside so make it look nice.

Now that your nest is taking shape, it's time to work on the interior. The reason I said you would need comforters is that they are usually very fluffy blankets and make great cushioning for the floor. You want to make sure it's comfortable or she won't want to stay in it very long. Lay the thickest, fluffiest blankets that you have down on the floor. I used three or four comforters as my floor and it was very comfortable. You don't want to use an air mattress unless it can take up the entire area. Lastly take the pillows that you have and lay them around the perimeter of the nest. These will be used as a backrest and as headrests if you lay down later.

So about now you are probably wondering what the television is for. I had a television that was mounted to a stand and it made for a perfect viewing angle. I found a really nice video of a beach with the waves crashing on the shore and played it on the screen. You can choose whatever scene that best fits your mood. For example, you can have a rain storm and the nest can be your place of refuge. One issue I ran into was that YouTube doesn't repeat the video and I didn't want to ruin the mood by getting up throughout the night to start the video over. A quick search online and I found a few sites that provided a free service of auto reload. A couple of the larger ones are www.youtuberepeat.com, www.listenonrepeat.com and www.youtubeonrepeat.com. All of them seem to work reasonably well.

Now that you have it all setup, all that is left is the refreshments. For presentation purposes and for ease of access to them have the drinks already in the nest when she arrives. We are both wine drinkers so I used wine glasses without stems so that they wouldn't tip over as easily. Try to minimize the amount of time that you have to leave the nest and in turn maximize that amount of time that you spend with her. I had already committed to making dinner, which is how this all got started, so I had to get up to prepare the food. A better choice may have been to order takeout so that once we got into the nest we could stay there. You definitely want to eat and drink in the nest, don't serve dinner at the table. Remember, you took the time to create this loving, safe place and now it's time to use it.

7 FACEBOOK

What You'll Need

- Computer or tablet
- Internet connection
- Facebook account

Why do flowers that get delivered to a person's workplace have more impact than flowers delivered to someone's house? That's because they gets to be the envy of all of their coworkers when they see the flowers and the same holds true with social media. Most people today have a Facebook account with all of their friends watching every post. Facebook is a great way to make your feelings known and make her the envy of her friends. Let's face it, most guys are not the romantic types and do not openly show their affection. This will be yet another time when her friends show their husbands or boyfriends what you did and say to them, "why don't you ever do anything sweet like that?"

The point behind this idea is to come up with a quote that speaks to you and your lover and not to simply share one that someone else has posted. So think about what you want to say and make it from the heart. It doesn't have to be something that will go down in history as the greatest saying of all time, it just has to be from the heart. One of the first ones that I created was, "Sometimes the best people come into your life during the most difficult times of your life." It was simple, from the heart, and something that was about our relationship. So reach into your heart and find something that resonates with your relationship. If you are not the type of person to be able to come up with your own, here are a few that you can use. Just don't tell her where you got them.

- Two hearts really do beat as one when you are in love.
- The saddest part of the day is when I have to say goodbye.
- Some people go their entire life without finding the kind of love that I feel for you.
- After meeting you, I now realize why all of the others had to fail.
- Sometimes two people come together during their darkest times and yet create a bond that can never be broken.
- You can't explain how or why love happens but you know it when it does.

The next step is to put it on a background image so that it can be posted to Facebook. Luckily there are several websites that will make this very easy for you. Some of my favorite are www.quozio.com, www.inspirably.com and www.quotescover.com. All of these have a place to name the author and that's very important because you want her to know that you came up with it and didn't just copy it. Remember this book is called, *How to Wow Your Partner*, not *How to Be Like Every Other Man With Your Partner*. My personal favorite is www.quotescover.com because they let you upload a picture to use and it has a lot of editing features. The nice thing about using your own image is that you can use one that was taken with the two of you. You can use a picture of the two of you, a special place that you two have been or even a picture of the flowers that you gave her in chapter two. A picture of a rose that you have given her can be used with great affect for your Facebook quote. Another way to make your quote is to use any image editor and simply add your text over the image. If you are familiar with image editing, you can have more options by doing it this way but it is not as simple as the other sites.

When posting your newly made love quote, make sure you tag her in the image. Tagging a person notifies them that it has been posted on her timeline so she that she will know to go and look at the post. It's important to note that tagging her allows her friends to see the post so be careful incase there is a reason that she doesn't want to share it. However when shared correctly it will make her the envy of her female friends. Post a new romantic quote every once in awhile – either when you think of a new saying or simply feel like sharing your feelings. Just be sure not to over use it or the wow impact won't be there.

Jaime T. McLain

8 MOVIE NIGHT

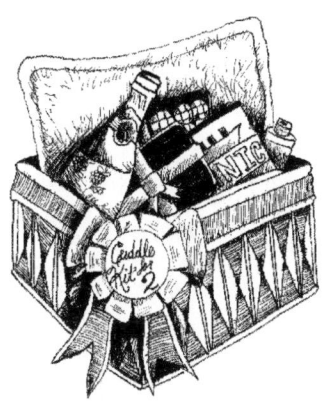

What You'll Need

- DVD or a streaming movie
- Basket
- Favorite beverage
- Blanket
- Snacks
- Small candles
- Red or pink fabric

If this idea involved simply renting a movie and watching it you wouldn't need this book. There is nothing wrong with having a quiet night watching a movie with your girlfriend. I love doing that myself but this is a "wow" book so lets take it up a few notches. I have to give credit to The Dating Divas, www.thedatingdivas.com, for this idea and it's one of my favorites. On The Dating Divas it is referred to as the "cuddle kit" (The Dating Divas, 2015). The items that I list are only a guide. As I keep mentioning, make it personal to the two of you. Listen to your heart and add items that mean something to you and to your partner.

For this you'll need a basket. I picked mine up at Michael's and it was fairly inexpensive. Any crafts store should have a basket that will work. To choose the correct size you'll need to know what you are planning on putting in it. For mine, I planned to put in a bottle of wine, two wine glasses, a bag of chocolates, a candle and a candle holder. Make sure you get one that is large enough to hold all of the items that you are planning on putting in there. The next decision is what style of basket. I choose one without a handle since I was planning on filling it with things and not carrying it around. It will be used as more of a display than a way to carry things.

While at the crafts store, pick up some red or pink fabric. You can use this to line the inside of the basket since most baskets come either without a liner or one with a plain color. This is supposed to show love, not that you are going on a picnic. When putting the fabric in as a liner don't worry, it doesn't have to be perfect. All you have to do it lay it in there, fluff it a little and you're good to go.

If you are a wine drinker, pick out a bottle with a romantic name. These days there are many fun and playful names of wines. Wine companies are getting very creative with their names and the days of wines with boring names are long gone. Some good examples are *Naughty Girl* by Von Stiehl Winery www.vonstiehl.com, *Hot to Trot* by 14 Hands www.14hands.com and *Fourplay* by Dievole. So head over to your local wine shop and pick out something fun, sexy and romantic.

Now for the snacks. This is the time to indulge in some foods that you wouldn't eat on a regular basis – don't try to be healthy. Go for chocolate truffles, small pieces of cheesecake or, my personal favorite, chocolate covered strawberries. Bite sized pieces work best so that you can feed it too her and add a little bit of sexuality to it. If you have to go healthy try things such as grapes, strawberries or small pieces of cantaloupe. Fruit is sexy, vegetables are not. Save them for your next dinner party, not your dinner date with your special someone. You also want to know what your partner likes and if she is allergic to anything, don't blow the evening by appearing insensitive and getting food she doesn't like. Both my girlfriend and myself are not big chocolate eaters so I stayed away from that and went with strawberries covered in white chocolate. The Rocky Mountain Chocolate Factory, www.rockymountainchocolatefactory.com, or Edible Arrangements, www.ediblearrangements.com, are great sources if you have them nearby.

Now it's time for a couple of candles. Try to go with red or pink candles to enhance the romantic atmosphere. Another thing to look for is the name. Some good examples from Yankee Candle, www.yankeecandle.com, are *MidSummer's Night*, *True Rose*, *Fresh Cut Roses* or even *Beach Walk*. It can be difficult to get a romantic name with a romantic color so I went with the name. Many of the red colored candles are for Christmas and didn't go with my romantic theme, especially since it was no where near Christmas time. Choose votive candles or the small glass jar candles. Remember you have limited space in the basket and you don't want the entire focus to be on the candles. If you go with votive candles as I did, make sure you get candle holders for them if you don't already have them.

Now it's time to put it all together. Start by taking the red fabric and placing it in the basket. Don't just lay it in there fluff it up some, you don't want it to be flat. Next set the bottle of wine or whatever beverage you are using into the basket. Place it so that the label can be read, after all you did spend time picking out an appropriate name. Place the wine glasses together and not on opposites sides of the basket. This symbolizes that your two hearts are together and not separate. Next simply place the candles and the snacks that you chose into the center of the basket. If you got an actual DVD, lean it against the back of the basket. Do your best to make it look nice and to be able to see everything that you put in it.

The last step is to place it in a central place where she will see it. If you have a coffee table, its probably is a great place because it's a central place in the house and right in front of the couch and television. You can place a folded blanket on the coffee table and put the basket on top of it. The blanket can later be used by the two of you to cuddle under. That brings everything together in one nice display of affection. Another nice touch is to print out the "Cuddle Kit" tag below, tie a ribbon through the hole and place it over the wine bottle neck. Customizing it with your names is an sweet touch.

Now you can both enjoy the fruits of your labor. After seeing this she will undoubtedly want to cuddle up with you throughout the movie and into the night. So pour yourself some wine, start the movie, pull the blanket over you, open the snacks and enjoy the closeness that you have created.

Jaime T. McLain

9 THE LIGHT OF MY LIFE

What You'll Need

- Pillar candle
- Computer
- Inkjet printer
- Printer paper
- Tissue paper
- Tape
- Heat gun
- Box (optional)

For this romantic idea we will be putting custom writing or a picture of you two onto a pillar candle; it will be one of those items that she will cherish for a lifetime. It is easy, unique and it is almost certain that she has never received one before. When I gave one to my girlfriend, she couldn't believe that I made the candle and had not ordered it on a website. This really isn't that difficult to do but the results will last a lifetime.

So to get started you will need a candle. You can go cheap on this because she will never know where you got it from and will almost certainly never light it out of fear of destroying it. You want to get one that is big enough to hold whatever text and designs you plan to put on it. Usually the tallest one that a crafts store has will work best. Get a neutral color as well so the writing or picture will stand out – avoid bright colors or black. I went with basic white and it looked great. Try to stay away from strong scented candles as well. You don't want to run the risk of her not liking the scent and therefore not putting it on display.

You will also need tissue paper, the kind paper commonly used to hide the present in a gift bag or used to wrap a shirt in when using a shirt box. You can find it at almost any store that sells greeting cards and gift bags. You will want to use the same color as the candle since you will be placing the printed tissue paper over the candle. Matching the color of the paper as closely as possible to the color of the candle will allow the paper to blend into the candle. White is the easiest color to match and allows the printed image to stand out and be easily read.

Now get on the computer and make your design – either a picture of the two of you, a meaningful phrase or combination. You can use any word processing applications such as Microsoft Word or Apple's Pages. If you are writing anything use a font that can be clearly read. I like the ones that look like handwriting because it gives the appearance that you wrote it and looks more personal but you have to be careful with them because they can sometimes be hard to read. If you are going to use a picture an image editor will probably work best. If you are using a picture remember to keep it simple so that it shows well on the paper. Black and white works well and it looks really good on a while candle. You can also use an image from the internet or clipart from the application that you are using to create it.

When you have a completed design then it's time to print it out.

Because the tissue paper is not ridged it will not feed into a printer without some help. To allow the printer to accept the tissue paper and prevent it from jamming the printer you'll need to attach it to a standard piece of printer paper. You will use the printer paper as a back to the tissue paper making it strong enough to be fed into the printer. When you are ready to print on the paper use an inkjet printer. An inkjet printer works better than a laser printer because an inkjet printer's paper feed is much slower than a laser printer's paper feed. This is important because the tissue paper will bunch up and jam on a laser printer. I tried this several times on a laser printer and could not get it to take the paper without jamming but it worked the first time and several times after that on an inkjet printer. To print your design you'll need to do the following:

- Pull the tissue paper tight over the piece of printer paper.
- Cut the tissue paper on all sides about an inch larger than the printer paper.
- Place the tissue paper over the printer paper and fold the sides over the back of the printer paper.
- Use the tape to secure the tissue paper to the back of the printer paper. Make sure it is as tight as you can get it.
- Use an iron on low heat to get any wrinkles out of the tissue paper being careful not to melt the paper.
- Insert the paper into the inkjet printer and print your image onto the tissue paper side.
- Check the printout and make sure you are happy with the results, repeat this process until you are satisfied with the printed image.

Now to actually put the printed image onto the candle. First you remove the printer paper from the tissue paper and then cut the tissue paper down to the size of the candle that you are using. Place the printed image over the candle to make sure the image fits on the candle. You don't want the image to be larger than the candle so if it printed too large, go back to the computer and reduce the size of it until it fits nicely onto the candle. Once you are certain that it fits the way you like it, wrap it tightly around the candle and secure it on the backside with a few small pieces of tape. Make sure it is as smooth as you can get it. You don't want wrinkles or air pockets in the paper.

For the last step you will need a heat gun or a hairdryer that gets very hot. If you don't have a heat gun you can buy one at any hardware store or Radio Shack. They are used by painters to remove old paint and in electronics to melt heat shrink around wires. This is where the magic happens. Turn on the heat gun and slowly melt the candle wax until you see it come through the tissue paper. It will appear as though the tissue paper is disappearing and leaving just the printed image. Continue to melt the wax through the entire image but be careful not to melt it so much that it changes the shape of the candle. I found that it worked well if you hold the heat on the candle for just a couple of seconds and then remove it. You can then determine if it needs more heat on that spot but if you hold the heat too long it will melt and distort the candle and you'll have to start over.

That's it except for the presentation. I went to my local craft store and picked up an inexpensive box that the candle fit into perfectly. It was nicely decorated and had a saying written on the outside that fit well with my relationship. Use the left over tissue paper to line the box with to make it look nice and not let it roll around. Carefully lay the candle in the box with the picture or writing facing out so that she will be able to see it as soon as she opens it. For an added touch, you can pick up a nice candle holder for it as well but a pillar candle looks fine without one as well. You've now created a memory and a keepsake that she will cherish for a lifetime.

10 DANCE THE NIGHT AWAY

What You'll Need

- A club, bar, restaurant or anyplace that has music and dancing

I know that dancing scares the hell out of most men and it scares me to but most women love to dance and love a man who will dance with them. If you are a good dancer that is great. But most of us guys are not and that is okay as well. Why would you not want to hold your partner close on the dance floor? It's a great feeling and a really good bonding activity. And just like everything in this book, the result comes more from the effort than the quality.

For an evening of dancing choose a location with a live band if possible. I find that it's more fun to dance with a live band than with a DJ. Bands tend to play more popular sing-along songs than DJ's so you are more likely to know the songs and you tend to be a little looser and more comfortable when you know the songs. When dancing just enjoy the beat of the music. Less is more here, don't overdo it or you will look out of place. Just move and keep looking her in in the eyes; that is all she really wants. If you're at a club, chances are that people are drinking and won't pay any attention to how good (or bad) of a dancer you are. Don't worry if she is a better dancer than you, it's okay to follow her lead. Just stay with her the best you can, it's about you two being together not a dance contest. If you are lucky enough to get a slow dance make the most of it. Remember that you are the guy so grab her tight with strong hands on her back. She wants to feel safe in your arms and she will reward you by coming in really close. Place your left hand strongly on her lower back and your right hand on her upper back. Your right hand can wander to run your fingers through her hair or to join your left hand. She'll love if you look her in the eyes while running your fingers through her hair. Don't just take my word for it, give it a shot.

Finally you can both take dancing lessons at a studio. This is a great way to build the connection between you and a great opportunity to hold her close. There are several types of dancing lessons for couples. Some good ones to start with are:

- Ballroom
- Hip-hop
- Swing
- Line dancing
- Salsa

There are probably many local dance studios that you can choose from depending on the type of dancing that you want to learn. Some popular national ones are the Fred Astaire Dance Studios, www.fredastaire.com and the Arthur Murray Dance Centers, www.arthurmurray.com.

I have taken salsa lessons with my girlfriend and salsa is a great style to do as a couple. It is not the easiest dance style but it is a lot of fun. Many Cuban restaurants offer inexpensive lessons so check around your local area for one that does. You can have dinner and drinks and then move to the dancing lesson. Salsa is a very sensual dance style in which the man takes the lead. She will love this and the two of you will be all about each other in no time. If you are new to this style take the beginners class. There is no need to try and impress her too much here, she'll love the fact that you are simply trying. Have fun with this and if you enjoy it continue the lessons. Make it a standing date night and advance to the intermediate class.

If she comes fro a different culture than you, then you can take a cultural dance class. This will show that you respect her and appreciate her and her background. If you want to do a cultural dance you obviously need to know what her background is or just do something that she has been wanting to do. Many cultures throughout the world have very beautiful dances. Some well known ones are:

- Irish Stepdance - Ireland
- Bollywood - India
- Folk dancing - United States
- Hula dancing - Hawaii
- Polka – Central Europe
- Native American dance – United States
- Bon Odori - Japan
- Maypole dance – United Kingdom
- Flamenco - Spain

11 SUMMER PICNIC

What You'll Need

- Picnic basket
- Blanket
- Cups, Plates, Utensils
- Picnic food

There is nothing like a romantic picnic on a beautiful summer day – just like in the movie where the man picks up the woman and they head out to some secluded field for a romantic picnic. Well, women have seen those movies too -- probably more times than you. Picnics are a nice way to spend some quality time alone with your partner. It is an opportunity for the two of you to talk or just enjoy each others company.

The first thing you'll need is the perfect location. While some people would prefer somewhere where there won't be a lot of people or distracting noises, other people may prefer a city park in the center of town. Picturesque places such as by the ocean, lake or river can be nice but remember that, depending on where you live, where there is water there are often mosquitoes. Many cities have parks and greenways that can make very nice places for picnics. These parks usually offer the added benefit of having picnic tables and garbage cans. You might want to pick a place near where she works so that you can surprise her for a picnic lunch. Choose a location that works for the two of you and make sure you check the weather before hand. Nothing ruins a picnic like a thunderstorm.

Probably the first thing you think of when you hear the word picnic is a picnic basket. Sure you can use a grocery bag, but to really make it memorable you should use a nice picnic basket. You can find them online at places such as Amazon, www.amazon.com, or on craigslist like I did. You want to make sure that it is large enough to fit the food, plates, utensils and drinks that you plan to bring. Many baskets come equipped with the necessary accessories and have specific places within the basket to secure them. A shoulder strap on the basket will make it easier to carry if there is a long walk to the location that you have selected. Unless you know for sure you will have a picnic table, make sure you bring a blanket to sit on. Even if there is a table available, it can be very romantic to lay together outside on a blanket, so you may want to pack one either way.

The food is the next area to think about. The standard picnic type foods such as sandwiches and potato salad work well. I recommend staying away from grilling hamburgers and hot dogs. Save that for a group picnic. This is about the two of you and grilling will take too much time away from that. You can make the sandwiches yourself or you may choose to pick some up at places such as Panera Bread, local deli or sandwich shop. If possible order ahead of time and take them to go. Stick with foods that are easy to eat and not overly messy. For example, soups do not make for a good picnic food because they are easily spilled. It's a good idea to pack a few bottled waters since you'll be outside most of the day and you do not want to get dehydrated. You can also pack your favorite bottle of wine or another favorite beverage. Don't forget to bring a bottle opener and glasses. Avoid using glass cups if you can, even if it's for wine, as they may break and be very difficult to clean up. A nice dessert rounds out a perfect picnic meal. Choose something you both enjoy but stay away from anything that would melt such as ice cream. Cheesecake, cupcakes or a couple of pieces of pie work well. They are delicious and are not very messy.

Once you are there, there are several things you can do in addition to eating. Take your partner for a walk and enjoy the sights and sounds of the outdoors. If you choose to go on a nature walk make sure you hold hands with your partner. Remember that this is about spending time together not about you fishing while she is reading a book. You can also bring a football, Frisbee or even a board game to play. Checkers, chess, Sorry or Parcheesi work well because they are easy to setup without a lot of little pieces to get lost. Choose any activity that you can enjoy together and that may be simply sitting and talking to each other or even taking a nap together.

Jaime T. McLain

12 MASSAGE

Massage can be a very sensual act with a person. To get a massage you typically remove your clothing and then a therapist rubs their hands over your body relieving the built up tension and stress. When I get a massage I get totally lost in it and forget all about the rest of the world for that hour. Why would you not want to share this amazing feeling with the person you love? For this idea I am going to offer two different options. The first one is going to be the personal massage where you give your partner a nice sensual massage. The second option is a couples massage where you both enjoy the experience together. Both of these are great things to share with each other and you can use both of these at different times.

Jaime T. McLain

PERSONAL MASSAGE

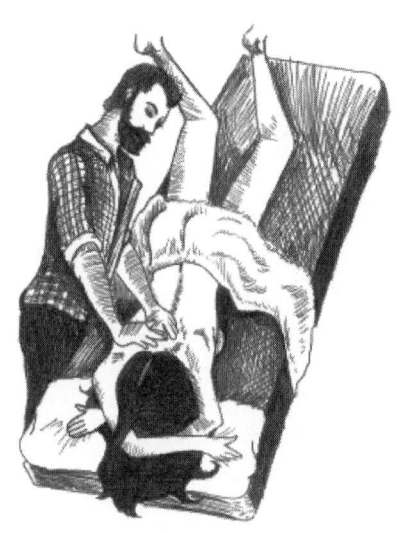

What You'll Need

- Bed
- Massage oil
- Candles
- Soft music

Giving your partner a massage is a great way to get close to each other and really relax her. She will love you for helping her relax after a long day or a stressful week. The reason that a massage is such a good show of affection is that it is all about the person getting the massage. You are taking the time and effort to do something that makes them feel good. All she has to do is lay there and enjoy the attention. I believe that the truest display of love and affection is when you do something for the other person and not for your own benefit.

The main purpose behind a massage is relaxation and stress relief, therefore a large part of making this happen is setting up the environment. For example, she is not going to be able to relax if there are kids running around or loud traffic sounds from a nearby highway. Make sure you choose a location that is quiet and that is not too bright. Closing the blinds or turning off some lights can really set the mood and provide a nice relaxing environment. Since most people don't have a massage table to use, a bed works quite well. It helps that most bedrooms are already setup to keep the light out for sleeping. Candles help set the mood as well and you can't have too many candle for a massage. The size, color and type of candle doesn't matter but they should smell good. A nice flower smell such as jasmine helps to produce the relaxing effect. Grab as many candles as you have and place them near the location that you will be performing the massage. The last step to set the mood is music. You want soft and relaxing music. Most big retailers such as Target and Wal-Mart sell relaxation music or you can download some from ITunes, www.apple.com/music or the Google Play store, www.play.google.com/store/music. Also make sure the room is generally clean. You want her to relax and not be focusing on the cloths laying on the floor or the food plates from three nights ago. Keep it clean so nothing distracts from the massage.

You will need some massage oil or something similar. You can use lotion but I find that lotion absorbs into the skin pretty quickly and therefore you need to reapply it quite often. This can also result in some dry skin rubbing which is not pleasurable at all. Oil on the other hand does not absorb as quickly and is very slick making for a nice smooth surface. I picked up an inexpensive bottle at a major retailer. I'm sure there are specialty stores that have more options but this worked fine. Just prior to using the oil, remove the cap and place it in the microwave for about 30 seconds. This will get it warm and feel much better on the skin. When you place the oil into you hand to apply it, make sure it's not to hot. Never put oil onto her when it's too hot, you certainly do not want to burn her.

Now to get her ready for the massage. I like to escort her into the room where you will perform the massage. Take her by the hand and lead her there. If she says anything simply put your finger on her lips and say, "shhh." She'll love the mystery and the fact that you are taking charge. As long as it's done with respect, even independent women occasionally like for the man to take control and this is a perfect time for it. Now once you are in the room, if you are this far in to your relationship and feel comfortable doing this, undress her. Just undress her slowly and always look into her eyes while you are doing it. Now have her get onto the bed facedown. It's optional for you to undress but I highly recommend it. What I find works nice is undress down to your undershorts for the massage and then if it progresses further -- and it probably will -- you can remove those after the massage. But at the beginning it's nice to not give the impression that it's all about sex, because it's not.

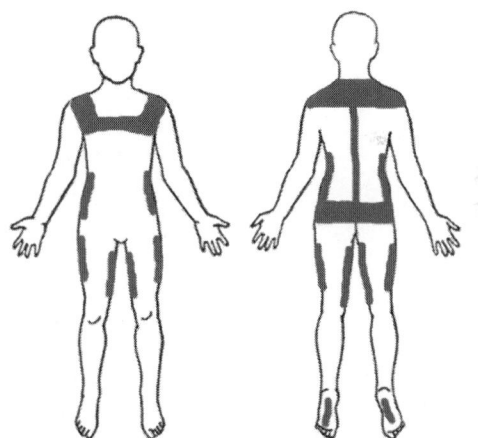

Now pour some oil onto your hands and start the massage. I'm not going too deep into how to give a massage, you can get that elsewhere, but I will give a few tips. People like different types of massages, hard, soft, deep tissue, etc. I like to go on the softer side. She can always tell you if she wants it harder but you don't want it to hurt her. Focus on the areas that typically get sore such as the upper back and the lower sides. Don't shy away from the buttocks, it's a large muscle that feels really good massaged and it also helps to get her in the mood but don't go there too fast. Take your time and really massage her back, arms and legs. Legs get really sore from standing and walking all day and feel great when massaged. The inner thighs also feel especially nice when massaged. Massage her feet as well, she'll love it. Remember to rub the underside of her foot. Women's shoes do a lot of damage to their feet so she will really enjoy that. If she regularly wears uncomfortable shoes take your time and don't rush things. If at some point you want her to flip over, the same rules apply.

It's good to have some clean towels nearby to wipe off the oil after the massage. A massage can release toxins that were being stored in the muscles so a glass of water after the massage is recommended to help flush these out. Enjoy the time together and the closeness that you two will undoubtedly achieve with this act.

COUPLES MASSAGE

What You'll Need

- Massage parlor or spa

Since a massage is so wonderful wouldn't it be great to enjoy one together? A couples massage is a great way to relax and unwind together while creating a special moment for the both of you. Not all massage places have a couples room so make sure you call ahead and verify that they have one. Not all couples rooms are created equal either. A couples room simply means that two massage tables are in the same room. I have seen rooms where you are both in there but not near each other while other couples rooms are configured so you're close enough to hold hands while getting the massage. I prefer to be close to the person I am with, it just seems to help build the connection. Calling ahead or going ahead of time to take a look at them will help you decide. Choose a location that has the type of room and atmosphere that you are interested in (and fits within your budget).

When you book your session, they will mostly likely want to know what type of massage you are interested in. Unless you already know a type that you both like, I recommend keeping it simple and going with the basic massage. Here is a basic overview of the most popular types of massage.

- **Swedish** – Swedish massage is the most common type of massage given in the United States. Since it is what most American's think of when they think of a massage, you may see it listed as simply "Massage." It is a general purpose massage that is very effective at reducing stress. If you don't know what type your partner likes, you are safe to order this type.

- **Hot Stone** – As the name implies, hot stone massage involves heated smooth stones that are placed on the body to loosen muscles. The concept is similar to using a heating pad on sore body parts. Oil is usually applied to the stones so that they can move smoothly over the body while the therapist applies pressure. This is a good choice for people with muscle tension or people who tend to get cold during a massage.

- **Deep Tissue** – Deep Tissue massage uses harder pressure to massage painful muscles. This is a good type of massage for people with chronic muscle pains such as the lower back. Not everyone likes the extra pressure so make sure you know what your partner likes before choosing this type of massage. If you don't know what she likes, stick with a Swedish massage.

- **Shiatsu** – Shiatsu is Japanese for "finger pressure." The Shiatsu style is when the masseuse uses his or her fingertips and palms to provide pressure at the acupuncture locations on the body. Since the fingertips are used instead of the entire hand, it results in more directed pressure feeling than other types of massage.

- **Sports** – A sports massage is usually used to help or prevent an injury. You don't have to be an athlete to get a sports massage but it is not a romantic massage and not appropriate for date night..

- **Aromatherapy** – Aromatherapy is a complement to the massage. Aromatherapy uses scents to create relaxation and stress relief. It helps create a nice atmosphere but the relaxation or stress relief usually comes from the massage.

Now enjoy your massages together. You've done all of the work now it's time for both of you to enjoy it. Try and let go yourself, this is one event that you can enjoy as much as she can. After the massage has concluded, make it an evening and go to a restaurant for dinner and drinks. She will likely ready to take on the town with the love of her life.

13 THE NOTEBOOK

What You'll Need

- A notepad, journal or journal software
- Time and patience

This idea is similar to the novel and movie, *The Notebook*. The story is about an older couple in a nursing home. The woman has Alzheimer's and cannot remember anything about her life. The man reads to her daily from a notebook that chronicled their love affair. From time to time she remembers hearing the story before but generally does not remember it or know that he is her husband. He took great effort to write very detailed accounts of their love but she thinks it is simply a touching romantic story not realizing that it is their story. As we get older your partner will look back on this gesture and remember the love that you put into it, just like the husband in *The Notebook*.

The idea came from my sister after she heard all of the romantic things that I was doing for the new love in my life. She commented that it was an amazing story and I should write it all down and present it to her later. That became my version of *The Notebook*. Doing this will take a lot of time, patience and diligence. This is not one that you will prepare for in the afternoon and present it during your dinner date. This idea will take months and possibly years to complete but it will be a very romantic gesture of documenting your courtship.

How it works is you to write down the details after every date, every special event, every sweet text or phone call, etc. It's a log of everything that has happened in your relationship. You can use something as simple as a physical notebook and pencil but I would recommend some sort of software or tablet application for a couple of reasons. First, if you have an application on your phone, you can add the details immediately while the event is still fresh in your mind. Also most software that has internet access will allow you to add entries from multiple devices so you can use your laptop, phone or tablet. They usually have the added benefit of having a backup incase something happens to your laptop, phone or tablet. Finally, keeping a digital notebook allows you to easily make it into a book. I used a program called Day One, www.dayoneapp.com, and was very happy with it. A quick internet search will provide you with many more applications to choose from.

Try to include as much detail into the entries as you can. Your memory will likely fade as time goes by and details of past events will be appreciated by both of you at a later date. Feel free to document your feelings as well, but stay positive. This is not the time to mention that you were upset because she was late but it is appropriate to say how much you missed her. Take a lot of pictures and add them too. Pictures are a great way to relive the memory. If I had forgotten to take a picture while on a date, I would go back to the place we were and take a picture of it later. Even though it wasn't a picture of the two of us it did add a nice touch to the notebook entry and help us to remember that night. You can also take screenshots of any text messages that you receive. I would get really sweet texts during that day and I would take a screenshot and then add that to the notebook. Add anything that you want to remember that pertains to specific dates, your relationship or how you feel about your partner.

The reason you are doing this is to surprise her with it at some later point in time. So you'll need to determine how we will present it to her and when. Let's start with the question of what you are actually going to give her? You don't want to open your laptop and show her some boring software program that you've been using and you certainly don't want to hand her some wrinkled up paper that you've been jotting down notes on. As I have said throughout this book, this is how to WOW your partner, not how to be like every other guy. One of the nicest ways to present this is to make it into a physical book. Thee are services such as Lulu, www.lulu.com, or FedEx Office, www.fedex.com/us/office, that can take your digital copy and make it into a book for you. I like to make each day, date, or special event a separate page. Think of those large coffee table books you see on special at your local bookstore. We are not trying to save paper, we are making a visual and written account of your love for someone special. It will be a really unique and nice keepsake that she can keep forever and share with her friends and family.

So when are you going to give it to your partner? How long do you need to document everything you do? Only you can answer this and I struggled with it some too. The end result took you a long time to create and it is best to give it to your partner on a big day or at a special event.

Some suggestions include:

- 1 year anniversary
- Engagement
- The day you move in together
- Wedding
- Honeymoon
- The arrival of a child

The amount of time required to put together a great book will be dependent on when you started it and at what point you want to give it to her. I would recommend a year or more but that depends on your courtship. If you think about it, keeping a journal for three months is not nearly as touching as keeping one for a year or even two years. So take your time and she'll be happy you did.

14 OPEN WHEN

What You'll Need

- Index cards
- Envelopes
- Computer
- Printer
- Pen or pencil in lieu of a computer

"Open when" cards are a gift that will make her think of you throughout an entire year. This is a simple idea that won't take much time to make but it will allow you to virtually be with her and be connected when she needs you. All you need is some envelopes, index cards, a computer and printer if you want them to look nice plus a list of important events or times when you think she will need you.

Here are some ideas for the cards. You can, and should, come up with your own as well. Anything that speaks to you your lady or your relationship. It can be when your favorite sports team gets eliminated from the playoffs or when she is craving Chinese food.

Open When:

- You get home tonight
- Valentine's Day
- Christmas
- One year anniversary
- You miss me
- When you need to know how much I miss you
- You are feeling sad
- You are feeling lonely
- Your birthday
- You are mad at me
- When you need a laugh
- You can't sleep
- You had a bad day
- You want to buy me a gift but don't know what to get

To make them simply open your favorite word processing software and change the page setting to the index card size. For Microsoft Word, simply click on File, Page Setup and change the paper size. Avery labels, www.avery.com, are very popular for printing and they come with details on how to print them correctly on their index cards. The index cards are going to be your answers. For example, "Open when you are feeling lonely" would have something written on the card that makes her feel better. Possibly you explaining how much she means to you or that you will be with her soon. Do this for each card that you have identified. If you have good handwriting or are crunched for time, you can also hand write the cards. Feel free to add some personal touches such as hearts, kisses or personal symbols to the cards. These can be hand drawn, computer clipart or even stickers.

You can use any envelope that fits the size of the index cards but I recommend making them look nice. I purchased some thank you cards that had really pretty envelopes from my local store. I simply threw the cards away and used the envelopes. Red envelopes work nice but white will work as well. You can use your computer and printer to write the "open when…" on the envelope or as with the cards, you can hand write them. Here's a good example to get you started.

Envelope:

Open when you are lonely.

Card:

If you have opened this card it is because you are feeling lonely. Sweetheart, there is no need to feel lonely because I am always with you. We are part of each other and my heart beats for you. Call me right now regardless of what time it is so that I can tell you how much I love and miss you.

Now you can put a rubber band around them or a nicer look is to use a ribbon to secure them. I find it's best to give them after a night out together such as dinner or a movie. Make sure your partner is in a good mood and that they are not upset with you about anything. This is not a gift to say you are sorry, it's an expression of your love for them. Now you have created something that will keep you in your partners heart for a long time to come.

15 WHAT'S IN A LABEL

What You'll Need

- Computer and printer
- Stick glue
- Bottle of wine
- Razor blade or knife
- Scissors
- Restaurant willing to play along

The goal for this special evening is to make it one that she will cherish for a long time to come. Since my girlfriend and I like the same kind of wine we drink it often when we go out. That made for the perfect opportunity to "wow" her by creating a unique custom wine label that is served to her in the restaurant. If you don't drink wine this can be used on beer bottles or any drink with a paper label but since a restaurant typically presents a bottle of wine to the guests to look at prior to opening it, it makes for an elegant way to surprise her.

The first thing to determine is the best location. I choose a restaurant that we frequented a lot. Since we had developed a relationship with the employees they were more than willing to help. Also we had been there often enough that I knew what wine they carried and could determine the size that the label needed to be. I had heard somewhere that it was illegal to bring in alcohol from outside of a restaurant so to avoid the potential of breaking any laws I planned to purchase the wine at the restaurant. Arrive early so that you can let them in on your plan and have the original label removed.

Before you arrive at the restaurant there are a few things that need to be accomplished first, such as making the new label. Microsoft Word allows you to make a nice label with very little effort. When making the label anything goes. Wine bottle labels come in all different sizes and can have anything from pictures to just simple words on them so anything that you like can work here. The only thing that I would strongly recommend is to make it very personal. Print your names on the label in a large font along with the date and location in a smaller size font. It's also nice if you come up with a cute name for the wine such as "Our Time," "Love Potion" or "Two Hearts." Use your imagination, it's all about how you feel about her. Add some hearts to it using the clipart function and a border to really make it stand out.

Here's an example of a label but make yours about you and her. The more personal the better.

So now that you have a label and you know where you are going to present it, you'll need to remove the label from the wine bottle. The easiest way is to soak the label in a sink of warm water. Let is soak with the label submerged for several minutes. After the soaking it should come off very easily. A razor blade will help and remove any residual glue or stubborn parts of the label. Once the label is off, dry the bottle completely so that the new label will stick well.

Take the new label that you have created and cut it down to the correct size. You'll need to put glue on the back of the label. I used stick glue because it was easy to get glue on the entire back and it doesn't soak through the paper like liquid glue tends to do, but use any glue you have on hand. Make sure you at least get the edges and corners so that it stays on the bottle. Place the label with the glue applied on the bottle and give it a few minutes to dry.

You can have the restaurant present it as they normally would or you can be the one to present it to your partner. Whichever you choose, make sure it's presented like a fine bottle of expensive wine. If you present it, lay it on your arm and put it in front of her and ask if it is acceptable. At this point she will probably start crying -- at least my girlfriend did -- followed by expressions like "Oh my god" and "I can't believe this." Enjoy the wine or whatever drink you used. She will most likely want to keep the bottle as a keepsake and you are the king for a night.

16 PUZZLE PIECES

What You'll Need

- Cardboard or poster board
- Photograph
- Glue
- Razor knife or scissors

A surprise is a lot of fun. Anticipating the surprise can sometimes be even more fun. For this one you'll make your own custom romantic puzzle to give her but you'll add a twist to it. Think about having a puzzle without the picture on the puzzle box. She will love the anticipation of not knowing what it is until it's complete. This is a creative, fun and different way to romance your partner and it will bring a big smile to her face.

First lets talk about the picture since you will need this regardless of which method you use to create the puzzle. You can use a picture of the two of you or perhaps a place that you have been. Choose something that is sentimental to the both of you. You can also really wow her by adding a custom message to it. What's great about adding a message is that she won't know what it says until the puzzle is complete. I chose to use a picture of a place that I was going to take her to as a surprise. When you've chosen your picture, use an imaging program to add your message to it. I added a message telling her when and where we were going there. Both Microsoft Windows and Apple's OS X come with free image editing software that you can use. Once you have your picture complete, print it out on photo paper or take it to a photo processing store for the highest quality.

At this point there are a couple of different ways to finish your custom puzzle and I'll explain both methods. The first method is by doing it completely by yourself. For this you will need a piece of cardboard large enough for the picture and without any fold in it. You can get a poster board from any major retailer or the top of a pizza box will work as long as it's clean. Take your picture and place the glue on the back side of it. I found that glue that comes in a spray can works best but stick glue works well too. Once you have glued the backside of the picture place it on the cardboard. Place a heavy object on top of the picture and let it dry overnight.

One the glue is dry, use the razor knife or scissors to trim the outside edges of any excess cardboard. Now place the cardboard and picture combination on a flat surface with the picture facing down. Use a pencil or dark marker and draw the puzzle pieces. Make the pieces have the standard interlocking tabs that you are use to seeing in puzzles but don't make it too complicated. If you use different shapes on the pieces it will make it too easy to put the puzzle together. You want to make them look standard so that it's a challenge to finish the puzzle. Once you have completed drawing the pieces, use your knife or scissors to cut out the pieces.

The second method is to have a company make the puzzle for you. I used Shutterfly, www.shutterfly.com, but just about any place that prints photos such as Wal-Mart, photos.walmart.com, can make a puzzle picture for you. You'll need to allow them a few days to make it and ship it to you but they usually produce high quality puzzles for a nominal fee. Having it made by a company will most likely create a higher quality keepsake than doing it yourself but taking the time and effort to do it yourself may mean more to her. You'll have to decide on which option you want to use. Most of these companies allow you to edit the photo and write a message right on their website. You can also have it delivered in a standard puzzle tin for extra effect.

Now that you have your custom photo puzzle you can decide on how and when decide you want to present it to her. You could simply give it to her at dinner but remember when I said anticipation can be a good thing? I had the puzzle together on my table and I would give her a different section of the puzzle every time I would see her. This built up the curiosity because it took her a while before she could read the message. It also made her to want to come over more often so that she would get more sections to put together. Make sure to give her sections of the puzzle as opposed to random pieces so she can start putting it together and trying to see what it is. Now let the fun begin!

17 HAMMOCK

What You'll Need

- Hammock
- Stand or hooks

I simply love hammocks. Just the thought of laying in a hammock while it slowly sways with the gentle breeze instills a sense of calm and relaxation in me. This one is a little less about the "wow" factor and more about spending some quality close time together. This is an easy one to setup but unless you already have a hammock, it will cost you some money. It doesn't necessarily need to be your hammock. I have used hammocks at parks and hotels but they can be hard to find and it may not be as quiet and personal as you would like.

If purchasing a hammock, make sure you get one that can hold the weight of two people. Many hammocks only support the weight of one person so take the time to choose correctly. You may need to pay a little more for a two-person type but it's sure better than crashing to the ground. When looking for a hammock there are a few different types that you can choose from.

- **Spreader type** – This is probably what you are use to seeing at pools and backyards and it's my personal favorite. The spreader type uses a piece of wood to spread the ropes apart at both ends. This keeps the hammock flat and allows for more surface area. It also makes it easier for the both of you to get on and off.
- **Venezuelan or Jungle hammocks** – These were the first type of hammock that were developed. They came out of the jungles of South America where people slept on them to keep them off the wet jungle ground. This type does not keep the hammock open and instead curls up around you. This is great for cuddling but it can be uncomfortable for two people since it is next to impossible to not be on top of each other.
- **Portable or camping** – These are usually small so that they can fold up into a neat little bag to be transported. These can be good to take to the lake and enjoy the outdoors together but be sure to check the weight requirements. Note that most of these are made for one person.

The next thing that you need to think about is how will you hang the hammock? For home use I find a hammock stand to be a good way to go since it can be moved around the yard. Just like with the hammock, make sure the stand is strong enough to hold two people. If you have trees close enough to each other or want to take your hammock somewhere, you'll want to get some hammock tree straps. These are thick straps that go around a tree and hold up the hammock. The straps can be moved up or down the tree depending on the terrain or how high off the ground that you want to be. They can also be adjusted for various thicknesses of trees or to compensate for trees that may be a little too far apart and of course they do not damage the tree. Most parks do not allow you to screw a hook into their trees so hammock straps solve that problem.

In most cases you will want to make a day or evening out of this. If you are using a hammock at home, make dinner for her first and then take her to the hammock. Things are always more romantic when there is an entire evening of things planned. If you're going to a park, combine this with the picnic chapter. When you are ready, just climb into the hammock together, wrap your arms around her and let your cares fade away.

18 COOKING

What You'll Need

- Recipe
- Kitchen
- Pots, pans, etc. needed to make dinner

Cooking is a great way to spend some quality time together. Even if you are not a cook, virtually anyone can follow a recipe. I have found that I am a horrible cook unless I follow a recipe but when I do, dinner comes out very good. Good recopies are easy to find on the internet. Most sites come with reviews from people that have tried the recipe so you can get a good idea on whether it's good or not before you make it for your lady. Some popular ones are Big Oven, www.bigoven.com and All Recipes, www.allrecipes.com. Some famous restaurants such as The Cheesecake Factory, www.thecheesecakefactory.com/about-us/our-recipes/ and Red Lobster, www.redlobster.com/kitchen even post their recipes online now.

Cooking can be done by you or with the both of you doing the cooking. Both are great fun but have different meanings. Cooking for her sets up a romantic evening where you take care of the food, the table and the atmosphere. Obviously choose something that she will enjoy but also choose something that challenges you to make it. Making spaghetti does not impress her nearly as much as preparing Chicken Masala. Yes I was able to make a pretty good Chicken Masala with absolutely no cooking experience. One of the hardest things that I have found is estimating the amount of time it takes to prepare the meal. You definitely want to start the dinner before she arrives because you don't want to spend your entire date in the kitchen and not paying attention with her. You will want to set a nice table with nice plates and candles. Make it a romantic experience and not just making dinner and eating it on the couch.

Cooking with her can be romantic in a fun and playful way. To cook together choose a recipe that is not too difficult. When you cook for her difficult impresses but when you cook together you don't want it to be so difficult that the focus goes only on the food preparation. You want this to be fun and playful. Make sure you have all of the ingredients, pots, pans and utensils that will be needed already out and ready when she arrives. It's best to assign portions of the meal to each other so that neither of you are confused on what you are responsible for. For example you can assign her the salad, pasta and vegetables while you work on the main dish, potatoes, and dinner rolls. Try to work side-by-side and play. Offer her a taste of what you are making, take a taste of hers without asking, put some mashed potatoes on your finger and offer her a taste but at the last minute put it on her nose. Then you can give her a big kiss and get some of it on you. Those kind of things are fun and make it a great night. If she's standing at the stove, come up behind her and put your hands around her waist and give her a kiss on the neck. How the dinner comes out is secondary to how much you play during the preparation of it, so enjoy the fun of doing this together.

Jaime T. McLain

FONDUE

What You'll Need

- Fondue pot
- Fondue food

Fondue is one of my favorite date night stay at home dinners because it takes a while to cook the food which allows you to spend some quality time together. Also there are so many tasty foods that can be cooked in a fondue pot that is makes for a fun evening. Making fondue on the coffee table in the living room works well so that you can watch a movie while you are cooking and may be a nice change from the dinning room.

There are two main types of fondue pots, electric and ones that use a fuel source such as Sterno. I prefer the electric pots because they heat up more quickly, cook the food faster and are generally easier to set up. The fuel-can type are good for cheese fondues and to just keep things warm but are less effective at cooking the food.

There are also three main types of fondue cooking; oil or stock, cheese and dessert. Oil fondue is one of my favorites types of fondue. You simply fill the fondue pot up with vegetable oil and wait for it to get hot. You can also use beef or chicken stock instead of oil. I use stock since it splatters less and has more flavor than oil. Add some onion, garlic and other seasonings to flavor it up. Do not use a fuel can type of pot with oil -- it will not get hot enough to cook the food. For the oil or stock type you can cut up chicken, shrimp, or tenderloin steak. You want soft, tender meats to use with fondue. New red potatoes cut up into smaller bites and assorted vegetables round out a nice dinner. Put the potatoes in first as they will take the longest to cook.

For cheese fondue, you melt various cheeses in the bowl. Use cheeses such as Swiss, American, Gruyere or Comte. They taste great and melt easily. Add a little cornstarch to the melted cheese to help thicken it but use it sparingly, too much and it will be too thick to dip things in. You can add about a cup and a half of dry white wine or other liqueurs for flavor as well.. For dippers, harder bread such as Italian or French bread works well. For other dipping items you can use just about anything but broccoli, cauliflower, carrots and pears work really well.

Here is the recipe that my friends came up with and it worked very well.

- 1-2 Quarts of chicken stock
- 4 Cloves
- 1 Onion, peeled, halved and studded with the 4 cloves
- 3 Shallots, unpeeled
- 4 Ounces of whole fresh ginger, peeled and minced
- 3 Whole garlic cloves, peeled and smashed
- 1 Cinnamon stick
- 1 Green onion sliced
- 4 tbsp. of Soy sauce
- ¼ Orange peel
- 1 Pinch of Red Chili flakes
- Place all in cheese cloth and soak in the chicken stock

A great way to impress your date is dessert fondue. You can use milk or dark chocolate, caramel or white chocolate. Choose the one that you and your partner prefer. Both my girlfriend and I do not like chocolate so we use white chocolate and it's very good. You can get the melting chunks at any grocery store and they are easier to use and melt faster than just getting a chocolate bar. Melt them in the pot and add a little heavy cream or liqueurs to make it a thinner liquid. I used Godiva White Chocolate Liqueur and it tasted great. Don't use too much or it will be too thin to stick to the food. Pretzels, strawberries, cookies or just about anything tastes great with chocolate fondue.

19 DINING OUT

What You'll Need

- Restaurant of your choice
- Imagination

Going out for dinner can be fun, it can even be romantic but just making a reservation does not make it a "wow" event. You might think that having dinner at a restaurant takes the romantic control out of your hands or limits your options but that is far from the truth. A restaurant provides you with many options to really wow her, and with it being in public the affect is magnified. The following are some ideas that make dinner with your special person even more special.

IN CONTROL

What You'll Need

- Restaurant
- Planning

As I've mentioned before, the thing I hear most from women is that they want a man to be a man. When asked to elaborate, they tell me that they want the man to make decisions on a date. Yes they usually want to provide their input but they want him to make the final decision. This one will have you being the man and her looking at you with those lovey eyes. Use this sparingly, she does want to give her input most of the time but sometimes, for one night, she'll gladly hand over control.

The concept for this one is that you take care of everything before she arrives. You order all of the food and drinks ahead of time so that all you need to do is enjoy each others company. Of course you'll need to have some idea on what she likes to eat and drink. This would not be a smart move for a first date. It's alright if you don't pick her favorite dinner but if you know that she doesn't like seafood then do not order shrimp pasta for example. As long as it is something she would enjoy you'll be okay. It's more about the surprise than it is the actual dinner, just don't make it a bad dinner.

This is all about preplanning. It helps if the restaurant has it's menu online. Grab your computer or smartphone and check out their website. If they do not have it online then you'll need to go visit the restaurant before your date. Once you have the menu, choose an appetizer and two main courses. Don't forget dessert and drinks as well. A nice touch its to order a single dessert with two forks and share it. Write that all down on a piece of paper or print it out on the computer so that it's easy for the restaurant to read.

Now that you have everything written down you'll need to arrive at the restaurant early. If she is meeting you there then just arrive before her, if you are picking her up then you'll need to go to the restaurant before you pick her up. Once there explain to the hostess or manager what you are trying to do and give them the paper. They will appreciate that you wrote it all down and you'll be their easiest customers for the evening because now they don't need to keep checking on you except to make sure the drinks remain full. Remember to tell them that you will not require menus and to ask for their most romantic table if they have one. The lack of menus will be her first clue that something special is going on.

When you both arrive at the restaurant try and stay cool. Act as though it is a standard dinner and that you haven't done anything special. It won't be very long before she realizes what is happening but I always try and act like I had nothing to do with it. Now you can enjoy the conversation, the dinner and each other. She'll love you for setting this up.

Jaime T. McLain

THE LITTLE THINGS

What You'll Need

- Restaurant
- One of the following: Flowers, Rose Petals, Sweets or Fruit

Making a special night at a restaurant doesn't always require a lot of work and grand ideas; sometimes just a small gesture is more appropriate. Spicing up a restaurant date can be done frequently since you don't want to go all out for every date. Occasionally you will need to arrive early to the restaurant but more often you can make the reservation online and fill out the box for special requests. I've used this several times with great success and excellent results.

As mentioned in Chapter One, flowers are always a good choice to give her on a night out. I like to arrive early at the restaurant and give the bouquet to the server to deliver during the meal. Another option is to have the flowers already on the table when you get seated. This can make for a nice surprise that your date usually does not expect. For either option, make sure you have a card in the flowers so that she knows that you are the one that put in all of the effort. The little card and envelope that usually come with flowers works fine here. It's cute and intimate -- no need to go for the big Hallmark card here unless it is a special occasion such as an anniversary.

For a different approach, sprinkle some rose pedals on the table before she arrives. This effect is straight out of a romantic novel and she will love you for it. My local grocery store has a really nice flower section that I have used quite often. It wasn't until recently that I found that they sell rose petals as well. It may just the petals that fell off of the many roses that they sell but it gave me this idea If your local grocery store doesn't sell loose petals, check with a florist. I'm sure they would love to get rid of some for a small price.

Another item that I like to have prearranged is the wine. Of course if you don't drink wine you can use any drink that the two of you enjoy. Tell the restaurant staff what type of drink that you would like and to have it ready on the table before you get seated. If it's wine, leave it in the bottle or decanter. Wine is best served when it's poured in front of the both of you. There is just something classy and romantic with watching them pour you a glass of wine. Pair wine with flowers and you have a winning combination that she will love.

Sweets are a good choice as well. Use something like chocolate covered strawberries. Strawberries are a very sensuous fruit and it is very romantic to have her eat one from your hand. Some other good options are chocolate mousse, chocolate cake, truffles or mini-cupcakes. There are many gourmet cupcake shops to chose from such as Gigi's Cupcakes, www.gigiscupcakesusa.com. If you're into healthy foods, grapes or oranges work just as well.

Just like the flowers, have the sweets on the table before you get seated. Request the restaurant staff to place them on a serving plate for better presentation. This will look much better than using the box that you purchased them in.

Jaime T. McLain

20 SCAVENGER HUNT

What You'll Need

- Computer and printer
- Fun ideas

Scavenger hunts are a fun activity for all ages and can be a great way to keep her thinking about you during an extended absence. For example, I put together a scavenger hunt when my girlfriend went home to see her family. I gave her the details the day before she left and she had two weeks to complete it. Working on the scavenger hunt meant she was thinking about me most of the trip. You can construct an item scavenger hunt where she collects items to bring back, or a photo scavenger hunt where she simply takes a picture of the requested items. If you do a photo scavenger hunt make sure you ask that she be in the picture. It not only proves she is there it is also a sneaky way to get more pictures of your sweetheart.

Start by researching what will be available at the location where she will be doing the scavenger hunt. For example, having her find a piece of lava rock if she is in Arizona or some Native American art in New York are not good ideas. You want to make the items fun, romantic and a little challenging. A picture of them in front of a heart or bringing back an item with a heart on it are good examples. Try to make them difficult enough that she can't complete the list in one day but easy enough that she doesn't ruin her vacation working on the list the entire time.

Use your computer and word processing software such as Microsoft Word to print out the list for her. Make the list fun and attractive by adding a border, her name, the date it needs completed by and maybe some hearts. Remember that she is going to be pulling this out of her pocket or purse regularly to look at it so make it nice. It's also a good idea to text it to her so that she has it on her phone. People seem to always have their phone on them but she may forget the paper. This will make it easy for her to take a glance while she is out.

Here are a few examples of a scavenger hunt list. The first one is the actual list that I used and she was able to complete all but two items.

A picture of you:

- In front of a famous place
- With a relative or friend that you haven't seen in at least 10 years
- With someone making a silly face (bonus points if they

- don't know why they are doing it)
- With both of your parents
- Holding up today's newspaper
- Looking into a mirror (must see your reflection in the picture)
- Kissing someone on the cheek
- On a kids ride (extra points if you actually pay to ride it)
- With someone with blonde hair
- In a sexy pose

Bring back:

- A napkin with the restaurants name on it
- A fortune cookie (extra points if the word "happy" appears in the fortune cookie note)
- Something that is older than you are
- A keychain with the city name on it
- A bag with the name of a store on it that I have never heard of
- Something with my name on it that you didn't write

When the scavenger hunt is compete, make an evening out of her showing you the items or pictures that she brought back. If you can, take her out to dinner or make dinner at home for her. Show her that you appreciate her playing along and that she took the time to finish it. She needs to know that it meant a lot to you for her to do this. If you don't show her that, it may be the last one she ever does.

21 GIFTS

What You'll Need

- The ability to listen

First let me be clear that this section is not about specific gifts for a big occasion. These are gifts to say "I love you" or "Just because I was thinking about you." Use these gifts sparingly, you don't want to give random gifts too often. Interestingly I learned from my girlfriend that material gifts did not mean as much to her as the other ideas in this book did. She appreciated the thought and effort but was not really into gifts with a few exceptions. My ex-wife was the opposite. She thought that romantic gestures were silly but get her an expensive gift and you were golden for a short amount of time. My point is that every woman is different so judge how often you should give a gift by your personal experience.

Gifts should come from the heart and be very personal. To wow your woman do not go and get a gift at the last minute or thoughtlessly pick out a random card at the local Hallmark store without reading it. Gifts for the person you love should take planning and a lot of thought. The gift should say that you care about her enough to listen to her and to pay attention to know what she likes or what she wants. Any splurge item that she might want but perhaps wouldn't buy for herself works very well. One of the best gifts that I got my girlfriend was a purse. Most guys would have shied away from getting a purse since we know very little about them but I heard her comment several times how she likes a certain brand but would never spend that much on herself. That's the kind of thought that should go into these gifts and I got the added benefit of smiling every time I saw her with it. Of course if it's expensive, you can use it for a birthday or holiday event.

Pictures of the two of you make great gifts. A nicely framed photo shows that the two of you together means a lot to you. There are several ways to give a picture but start out by carefully choosing the picture. You don't want to use one that she thinks she looks bad in. The first one that I used was a picture of the two of us at a hockey game. I know it doesn't sound romantic but the way she was looking at me in the picture and the way she leaned into me just made me feel great. When I told her how it made me feel, she replied that she felt the same about it. Pictures where you the two are holding each other tight also show that caring well. Don't use a cold or highly posed picture, use something with caring and warmth. You want people to look at it and say, "Awe, you two look so cute together".

There are many ways to get pictures these days but make sure you take the time to give her a quality one. If you are going to use your computer and printer to create it, make sure you use quality photo paper. Do not use standard printer paper or it will not look good. It will take away all of the shine that you are used to seeing in photographs. If you have access to a laser printer, use that over an inkjet. Laser printers are much crisper and dry instantly where inkjet printers can smear if they are touched before they are dry. When cutting the picture to fit the frame, take great care to make the cuts straight. You can also take your phone or storage card to a Wal-Mart, Walgreens, CVS or just about any camera store and they will professionally print them out for you for a small price. Some even let you send it to them using email or their phone application and then you simply go and pick it up.

One way to give a picture is to get a nice picture frame and put the picture inside it. Never give just a picture without a frame and always take the time to get a nice frame that complements the picture or reinforces it with a theme such as a coral frame for a beach picture. Personalized frames are great. Anything that says love, or together, or anything like that will be appreciated. You can get one personalized at Things Remembered, www.thingsremembered.com. You can find them in most malls. I purchased a keychain picture frame from there and had it engraved on the back with the date and the occasion. What's great about a keychain is that she will always have it on her and won't have to wait until she gets home to look at the picture of the two of you.

Jewelry is an option but you need to be careful since jewelry is very personal and means your relationship has reached a certain stage that she may not be ready for. Earrings are good for newer relationships followed by necklaces and finally rings. Stay with the romantic theme and choose hearts whenever possible if it matches her style. I don't believe that cost is as important as the thought unless it's an engagement ring and there are plenty of guides out there for that. If one of you are from Irish decent, the Claddagh is a nice option. The Claddagh is a traditional Irish symbol which represents love, loyalty, and friendship. The hands represent friendship, the heart represents love, and the crown represents loyalty (Claddagh ring, 2015). Just go more with what it represents and less with what it costs and you will be fine.

22 BEDROOM ROMANCE

What You'll Need

- Rose pedals
- Candles

What better place to be romantic than in the bedroom? This chapter is not about sex. These are just some little things that you can do to make your bedroom just a little less boring. Contrary to what you see in the movies, the average man's bedroom is not a romantic place for a couple -- but that doesn't mean it has to be that way. Through most of this book I have talked about how doing these romantic gestures in public makes a big impact. In this case it's about the two of you. If you are dating and not married, your girlfriend may feel awkward in your bedroom even if you two have been in there previously. It's due to the stigma that society has created for adult women who are dating but not married. These special touches will make it more of a shared space and a place where she feels safe and comfortable. It will help her to relax and show her that it is about the two of you being together and not about the sex.

Candles are always a good option for the bedroom. You can't have enough candles, they just make for a very romantic atmosphere. Try to light the candles before she enters your room -- it's not nearly as romantic if she has to stop and watch you light them. Lit candles makes for the perfect lighting. My girlfriend liked them so much that one day I didn't light them and she said, "What no candles? Is the honeymoon over?" She said it in a sassy, joking way but I got the hint. Make sure there are some on the tables near the bed but if that is not an option, anywhere will do.

Rose petals are great to add some romance to the bedroom. If you are going out for dinner, a nice thing to do is to place the rose pedals like a road from the front door, up the stairs and into the bedroom. When you get home she'll see the beautiful path and lead you right to the room. This doesn't work as well if you are making her dinner or watching a movie at home first because she'll see the petals the entire evening and it won't be a surprise. For the bedroom itself, make a heart on the bed out of the rose pedals. She will be so touched that she will probably start crying when she sees it. One thing to remember is that if you have a white comforter, make sure you lightly brush off the rose pedals before you get into bed, otherwise they will stain the comforter.

A new canopy for your bed can be fun and romantic. This combines the safety and comfort of the "Love Nest" idea with the romance of the "Fairy Tale." If you are lucky enough to have a four-poster bed, you can use the type that covers the entire bed. Find some fabric, sheets work fine for this, and lay it over the posts. Just like in the *Love Nest* chapter, you can use folder clips to hold the sheets together. You can also hang one from a ceiling fan over the bed. This creates more of a circular canopy instead of a large square one as with the four-poster bed version. You can use a large sheet for this as well or purchase one from places like Bed Bath and Beyond, http://www.bedbathandbeyond.com/, or Amazon. For an added touch I purchased some glow-in-the-dark stars from a local store and placed them on the inside of the sheets. She'll be seeing stars both in the canopy and in your eyes. Now enjoy the comfort of getting inside of it and cuddling up close to her.

Jaime T. McLain

23 CONCLUSION

Dr. Leo Buscaglia, University of Southern California professor and author said, "What love we've given, we'll have forever. What love we fail to give, will be lost for all eternity." Now that you have a good start on romancing your partner, keep in mind that this book and these ideas should be where you start, not where you end. Keep the love alive by surprising your partner with romantic ideas such as the ones in this book but don't limit yourself to these. Come up with your own or modify these with your personal touch. The point is to not let your relationship get too routine or boring. Make it a life long journey of showing them how much you love her and reminding her why she fell in love with you. Whether it's a quick dinner and back home to be with the kids or taking a romantic gondola ride in Venice, Italy, take the time to make it a little more special. Don't make her feel like it was a bother to you to be together. It's important to not lose that passion for each other. How often you do something special depends on the two of you, everyone is different. I was told about one man that left a love note on a Post-it on his wife's pillow before he went to work. He did this every day for years. Others will have dinner and a movie once a month. The point is that every couple is different but don't let it stop. It is much more difficult to rekindle the passion then it is to keep it alive in the first place.

Aside from the romantic ideas in this book, I have also presented a few general concepts that I believe to be true for the vast majority of couples. These are generalizations and I realize that they will not fit all people but I have found that they are accurate for most people. Lets review a few of these that are mentioned in the book.

- **Being the man** – In most couples there is a more dominant person and a more submissive person. The concept here is that the more submissive person usually likes the more dominant person to take care of the planning for dates or romantic encounters. The "wow" factor comes in when you can sit back and watch the events unfold. This can work both ways as well. For example, I am the more dominant person in my relationship but the other evening my girlfriend sent me a text saying that she was coming over that evening and I was to sit back and let her make dinner and provide a nice evening for me. Switching roles for the night was a fun change and made for a wonderful evening.
- **Romance not hookup** – This book is about showing the love and respect you have for someone, not about casual sex. Build a foundation for a life-long journey of love and happiness with your partner by repeatedly showing them what they mean to you. Do not use this for a "one night stand."

The strength behind this book and these ideas is to build a strong lasting bond of love, respect and admiration. It will only be successful if your feelings are real; do not try to project an image or feelings that are not genuine.

- **Surprise** – The element of surprise is very powerful in the "wow" factor. We usually enjoy a lot of "nice" evenings with our partners but adding a surprise can make it a life-long memory. They both have their place but when you intend to "wow" your partner, try to keep it a surprise and let the events that you have planned unfold in front of her eyes.

- **Personalize** – The ideas in this book came from my heart and my love for a specific woman. Use this as a guide and personalize them to fit your relationship or as a launching pad for ideas on your own. Think about what your partner means to you and what you think she would enjoy. For example if she likes to go dancing tip the band to dedicate her favorite song to her and have them announce something like; "Tim would like Lori to know that he loves her very much." If she likes to take baths prepare one for her. Place candles in the bathroom, play soft music, get some nice bath salts and leave her a note telling her that you love all the things she that does for you and that now she should take some time for herself. The options are limitless.

Have fun with these ideas. Nothing in this book should be a chore. Make every idea and special event that you create be fun to plan and execute. Don't stress on whether everything goes perfect or if your partner will like what you have set up. Nothing goes perfectly and as I've noted before, it's more about the fact that you are taking the time to show how much they mean to you than the actual execution. If you concern yourself too much with making everything perfect, you will be focused more on the plan then on her and may actually cause the event to go less smoothly then it could have. Once the plan is in place, take a deep breath and enjoy the evening.

Feedback is important to be able to grow and adjust these ideas. I would like to hear how your romantic ideas went – either ones from the book or ones you came up with on your own. As you try new romantic ideas let me know how you set it up and what the reaction was. I would appreciate any feedback you may have. I expect this list to continue to grow as the readers experiment with their own ideas. Send your feedback to romanticideasforguys@gmail.com.

ABOUT THE AUTHOR

Jaime McLain has worked in technology most of his career and currently resides in Raleigh, NC. He holds a bachelors degree in computer information systems as well as a masters degree in management.. Jaime also severed two enlistments in the United States Air Force before entering the private sector. When not working he enjoys playing the drums and driving his 1968 Mustang that he restored, spending time with his family and especially being with the special woman who inspired this book. Jaime has a son Jay, and two daughters, Angela and Samantha. He is also the brother to four older sisters. You can contact the author at romanticideasforguys@gmail.com.

REFERENCE

Claddagh ring. (2015, July 9). In Wikipedia, The Free Encyclopedia. Retrieved 15:05, July 10, 2015,
from https://en.wikipedia.org/w/index.php?title=Claddagh_ring&oldid=670704932

Cuddle Kit for Two: An Easy, Romantic Gift. (2013, March 7). Retrieved July 15, 2015,
from http://www.thedatingdivas.com/romantic-rendezvous/cuddle-kit-for-two/

Hammock. (2015, June 1). In Wikipedia, The Free Encyclopedia. Retrieved 13:37, July 10, 2015, from https://en.wikipedia.org/w/index.php?title=Hammock&oldid=664987848

Miller, Claire Cain. (2014, December 2). The Divorce Surge Is Over but the Myth Lives On. *The Ney York Times*. Retrieved From http://www.nytimes.com/2014/12/02/upshot/the-divorce-surge-is-over-but-the-myth-lives-on.html?smid=fb-nytimes&smtyp=cur&bicmp=AD&bicmlukp=WT.mc_id&bicmst=1409232722000&bicmet=1419773522000&_r=4&abt=0002&abg=0

HOW TO WOW YOUR PARTNER

Printed in Great Britain
by Amazon